DANUBE CANAL

PAGES 106–111
*Street Finder maps
1, 2 & 5*

PAGES 68–87
*Street Finder maps
2, 4, 5 & 6*

Stephansdom
Quarter

Hofburg
Quarter

PAGES 88–105
*Street Finder maps
3, 4 & 5*

Belvedere
Quarter

PAGES 142–157
*Street Finder
map 4*

D0977924

EYEWIT

VI